Make Money Online: Twelve Proven Methods To Earn Passive Income And Work From Anywhere in the World

Max Lane

Copyright Notice

Disclaimer

Can I Ask You a Quick Favor?

If you like this book, I would greatly appreciate if you could leave an honest review

Reviews are very important to us authors, and it only takes a minute to post.

Download Audio

This book is also available now as an audiobook.
Head over to www.audible.com or
Download on the Audible application

Other Books by Max Lane

Evernote: Master the Powerful New Way to Organize Projects and Optimize Productivity - Collect, Share, and Grow Ideas

Do you use Evernote?

Chances are you are missing out on some of the key functionality of the Evernote app. Sure you know that you can share notes between devices and put multiple types of media in a note, but how can you use Evernote's feature set to make your life more organized and streamlined? This book is a beginner's manual for learning how to use Evernote and get the most out of the application.

Find out more

In This Book You Will Discover

Twelve proven methods **to make money online**. Ones which are working right now, and will continue to work in the future. Each one is explained in simple, easy to understand language and are possible to do from anywhere in the world (provided you have a wi-fi connection)

Making money online is real! We live in exciting times, because there are now many ways to make money from home. Imagine if you could earn an income online, make money in your spare time, on your terms, and… **work when you want, where you want.**

Learn the tactics I used to **earn as much as $50 per hour** of my time, with nothing more than a computer and internet connection, **no prior experience required**. With the right type of go-getter type of attitude and persistence, this book will pay for itself a million times over! It's clear and actionable advice with helpful information and detailed, step-by-step methods for anyone looking for **real ways to make money online.**

- Analyzing Why People Fail Online - And What You Can Do Differently
- How To Get Started Making Money Online With No Experience
- Outsource Your Business And Have More Free Time
- How To Start A $10,000-a-month Business Thanks To eBooks

- Dotcom Millionaires Personal Secrets To Generate Passive Income
- Master All The Hacks That Will Help You Work Online And Generate A Life-Style Change
- Benefit from The Most Profitable Websites to Work Online
- Monetize Your Passion and Skills on The Internet
- Make Money Online While Travelling
- And Much, Much, More……

So whether you're looking for some additional income on the side.

Or you desire to leave your 9-5 job and have the freedom to live and work where you want.

Then Read On…...

Contents

From Minimum Wage To Financial Freedom Online

I'm Max Lane and I was born and raised in Boston. I dropped out of college and literally was three months away from graduation but I was working online on the side. I actually chose to dropout of college in order to burn the boats so to speak and then pursue entrepreneurship full-time. At the start this didn't exactly work out as planned so I took a customer service support job to finance my life.

I worked for three years in an organization with over one thousand employees and hated the job. For any of you that have a call center background of tech support or customer service support then you know that it can be pretty grueling because your talking all day and since it's a minimum-wage job you have no time. Your lucky to have off Christmas Day. As far as breaks, you're policed about going to the bathroom you know you better be sitting there and holding it. Basically it's just a very controlled environment. Customers are very rude you're getting chewed out by them day in and day out. They're angry and you can't say anything back to them. I was always having to resolve their problems and bosses treat you very much as an expendable. I'm sure that you guys know all too well about how you're not appreciated at all with most lower wage jobs.

I came to the realization that you can lose your nine-to-five jobs at any time. You can face any pain throughout your life because you are depending on a source of income which is not your own. It's the source of income related to someone else and you are depending on it, exchanging your time for money. Coming and doing your best efforts but then you will not get the loyalty from the company to keep you. They can decide to let you go at any point of time if they want to. This and hating my job motivated me to spend all my free time learning about making money online and investing my hard earned wages into learning and starting out.

Now three years later I've been able to do a lot of cool stuff. I made five thousand dollars in a single week and have been very happy to make a legitimate source of income online that has made me independent from the nine-to-five jobs.

You might be thinking that it's not possible for you. You tried, you failed, your not smart enough or you're too old. These are all excuses that hold you back. It's never too late for anybody who is suffering from his or her nine-to-five jobs to think about a legitimate business opportunity that they can start to make money online with.

Ask yourself. Why do you want to make money online? Is it so that you can have the freedom to go do cool stuff, spend more time with family, go travel, go on vacations, not have to work a nine to five job? Or is it to make some extra pocket money?

Whatever your reasons are, if you have reached the point where you are ready to start a new chapter in your life and make money online then read on.

Kindle Publishing - How To Profit With E-Books

Kindle publishing is still one of the easiest ways to start building an online business, especially if you don't have much tech skills. If your a relative newbie to online business and internet marketing then this is a great business model to learn. It's got a fairly fast learning curve compared to a lot of other businesses out there and it's not as complex. It's also great if you don't have that much money to invest. The reason why Kindle publishing is great is because you're leveraging Amazon which has hundreds of millions of customers at your disposal. Amazon still remains as the number one book retailer in the world and ebooks aren't going away. So when you understand the right strategy then that's what's going to allow you to consistently make money long term. This can be a transformational income stream for you.

Once you understand the Amazon search engine algorithms then you can tap into that. Then your also leveraging yourself because you don't have to write the books yourself. You can if you want or you can hire writers ghost writers to write the content for you. Then you can operate more as a publishing company where you're the one that's publishing the book and doing the marketing for it. In the same way, you might also leverage yourself by hiring a graphic designer to design the cover for your book. You can leverage a lot of the process and you can do it in a very inexpensive way.

The most important thing to consider when you're publishing a book on Amazon is the niche or market that you're publishing the book in. Oftentimes a lot of people make the mistake of thinking they have this amazing idea, that they want to write a book on and they spent all this time creating it. Then when they finally put it out there they find that it just does not sell. You can't try to reinvent the wheel or create a new market from scratch. You have got to identify what people are searching for, what's hot and what's making good money. There are ways that you can research that and see how well certain books are selling.

First you have to identify demand and research what's selling on Amazon. Amazon is one of the biggest search engines in the world. People go there and type in a keyword. They might type in, weight loss, or meditation, or law of attraction, or motivation, or whatever it might be. To give you ideas of a niche. Ask yourself, what is a problem that my book can solve? People often buy books to solve a specific problem or to gain a certain benefit. Your book has to meet the needs and the demands of the market. So doing the proper research is very important because you could publish a book in a niche or market that there's no demand for. If your trying to market and sell it but nobody really wants it then you're going to have a hard time.

Once you've identified the niche market you want to publish your book in then you need to optimize your book for specific keywords. When someone searches for that keyword, then they can find your book. Knowing the right keywords is very important. Certain keywords would be less competitive than others but if you do a better job at marketing then you can outrank a lot of the competition fairly easily. To find good keywords type your main niche keyword into the Google keyword tool to find related keywords. You can also type it slowly into the Amazon search bar and it will auto populate with relevant search terms that can more accurately define your book.

Once you have identified keywords you need to create the title. The title should be optimized and contain your main keyword. Don't make it too logical, try to have some emotion in it. The best titles offer the main benefit and intrigue people to buy the book. Think about how you're going to position your book in that niche market. If you can differentiate yourself from the other books out there that's going to be an advantage for you. There are many ways you can do that. It could be based on having more pages in your book, a more quality a book or a better cover that stands out. Or maybe it has more and information than other books. it could even be through the marketing by having more reviews than other books out there.

Now when it comes to creating the book, if it's something that you could do, then write it yourself or hire ghostwriters. Ghost writers are very common in the publishing world. A lot of books that you might see out there such as a book by Elon Musk or Donald Trump have used ghostwriters that are writing the books for them.

For ghostwriting services you can use websites such as. www.ewritersolutions.com or www.epicwrite.com

Next step is the cover and this has to stand out when people see it. It is very important in terms of getting people's attention. Try contrasting colors to what your competitors use. Also, use high quality images and designs. You can outsource designing the cover inexpensively on www.fiverr.com, for five or ten dollars. It's a good idea to order from a few different sellers just so that you can get some variety and then pick the one that you like the most, or you can even test them. That's the great thing about an e-book like this, is that you can actually test different covers. You could publish one book that has one cover for a week or two and see how it sells and then you can republish it with a different cover and see if that makes a difference.

Once you have all these materials, your ready to publish your book. Sign up for a Kindle direct publishing account (KDP). This is the platform that you can use. It's free to sign up for it and you just create a new e-book then enter in the details like the title, the description, keywords and the cover. The description should utilize good sales copy to convert the most customers. Make sure you have a good understanding of copywriting to help you with this. Then you make sure the book is formatted properly and upload it. Finally you set the price that you want to sell it at. Amazon typically will pay you a royalty from each sale for up to seventy percent. The money gets direct deposited into your bank account and they pay out every every thirty days.

The great thing about this type of business is that it's all relatively quick, once you hit the publish button your book will be live on Amazon available for sale within twenty four to forty eight hours. You can also make it available as a paperback. This is an on demand service, so you don't need any stock. When a customer orders your paperback, Amazon prints it. In KDP the option to publish a paperback version is linked in with the ebook. You just need to format your book and cover file to suit the requirements. There are some gigs on Fiverr that can help you with this.

When your book is live you must promote it and market it. This is what a lot of people neglect to do. They think that Amazon is just going to do everything for them. Marketing is what you really have to learn because long term this is what's going to allow you to really be able to make a significant amount of money online. There are a lot of books out there that are great books. But nobody knows about them because a lot of authors unfortunately are really bad marketers. The more sales you have, the better your books will rank on Amazon.

The most effective strategy is using PPC which is pay-per-click advertising on Amazon. This allows you to use sponsored adverts so you can actually pay to have your book show up next to similar books or in relevant searches. When someone clicks on the advert Amazon charges you. Facebook is also powerful when it comes to marketing outside of Amazon. With Facebook there are many strategies. There's having a fan page in the niche that you're in, it could also be a Facebook group or it could even be Facebook adverts. Build up your Facebook fan page, learn how Facebook works and start creating content for it. You can also publish adverts and promotions on Instagram, Twitter, YouTube and your blogs. Essentially you're building a brand that's going to attract people to you that you can then funnel to your book. You should also build an email list and build that relationship with them even further. Aim to diversify your streams of traffic because Amazon often change their algorithm for ranking.

Finally, you can use KDP tools such as KDP Select to make your book available for free for five days. This will encourage lots of downloads and in turn more reviews. KDP Select has a ninety day sign up period. I suggest you do it once and then take your books off it so that they are non exclusive. You can then upload them to www.draft2digital.com which will publish it in a lot of other stores. Just leave it and let it generate passive income.

How are you enjoying this book?
If you like it please share your thoughts and give it a review, thank you and enjoy the rest of the information.

Increasing Your Income With ACX

Audible/ACX is website that allows you to publish and buy an audio version of a book. Right now, the audio book business is booming and there is not much competition with only five percent of books available in audio version. If you currently have books published on Amazon, or are planning to then it is an easy and affordable way to turn your books into audiobooks and in turn increase your earnings.

The first step you need to take is publish your e-book on Amazon KDP (check the section on Kindle for more details). Once you have published it and it is live in the Amazon store head over to www.acx.com.

To add your title for sale proceed as follows. Inside there are four tabs. Go to add new title, you can search for your book here. Now you need to find a narrator, or if you have a decent voice and recording gear then you can do it yourself. Select one of the following options as suited to you.

I'm looking for someone to narrate my book
Or
I have audio files ready

Then click agree and continue. ACX will then pull your description from Amazon. You then need to add in your name, publishing year and categories. When selecting criteria for a narrator you can choose from male or female, language and voice style. Fill it in and then you just upload a couple of pages for them to use in auditions. Then click save and continue. Simple stuff.

Next is the distribution page. ACX will sell your book on Amazon, Audible and iTunes if you choose an exclusive deal. They are the best out there and it will give you better royalties to be exclusive with them so select that option. Then select how many words are in your book and Audible will calculate the estimated length. They estimate one hour to be roughly 9300 words. Always go for longer books when you write because ACX prices longer books higher, which is more money for you. The pricing scheme is as follows.

- Under 1 hour: under $7
- 1 - 3 hours: $7 - $10
- 3 - 5 hours: $10 - $20
- 5 - 10 hours: $15 - $25
- 10 - 20 hours: $20 - $30
- Over 20 hours: $25 - 35

Next you have the payment options. These are a 50/50 royalty split, or pay narrator. I suggest you pay the narrator up front. Narration is affordable, you can get a decent one for an offer of around twenty five usd per hour. Otherwise you are losing fifty percent on each sale. However if cash is tight or your not confident in your book selling then do a royalty share.

Finally you can choose how long for first the fifteen minutes to be available for review and also for how long to complete the book. Confirm everything then click to post to ACX. Narrators will then send their auditions to you for review. Listen to each one then make an offer. When they accept send them the manuscript.

When it's all done you will need to send payment and upload cover art. You should avoid stretching out your Kindle cover to fit because it looks low quality. Create new cover art that looks similar to the Kindle cover. You will also need to have great sales copy and keywords. These can be taken from your research.

Right now ACX do not offer any advertising services but it's a good idea to contact them for promo codes for your books. They will give you fifty. You can send these to your network and ask them to review your audiobooks. Better reviews will help you get ranked higher. Again focus on creating great quality content that adds value. Finally make sure you keep scaling your books. The more you have the more your income will grow.

How to Start Affiliate Marketing

Affiliate marketing in essence is receiving a commission on sales through referrals. For example you can recommend products like headphones that you already use every single day and a earn commission off of them. The great thing about it is that you don't need any products and you don't need to worry about shipping them out. The company takes care of all of that for you so it's less hassle, less headaches and no customer service. You just get a check at the end of the day.

It's really not that hard to get started. The best program to start out with is Amazon Associates which is the number one affiliate program in the world. First off you sign up and choose any product that Amazon sells. You can basically promote it with your links. Mostly affiliates put these links on their website or they put them in the description of their YouTube videos. If you have ever watched a tech review you will often see an Amazon link in the description. That I guarantee you is an Amazon Associates link and they are earning commission off of each product.

Now, how much commission can you earn? It depends on the product category.

So for example, you can earn a six percent commission for selling headphones. So six percent of a $350 set of headphones is $21. Honestly that's pretty good considering that you don't have to buy the product or ship it out and hold inventory. Basically, Amazon takes care of everything for you.

The most popular method of affiliate marketing with Amazon is to review products and then promote them via Amazon Associates. If you join Amazon Associates there are different rates for everything on sale. For example a vacuum can get you eight percent of every $35 sale. So you get $2.80 for every single vacuum you sell. Look around your house, look for stuff that is sold on Amazon. It doesn't have to be high ticket expensive stuff. However I do recommend that you promote high ticket items because obviously the bigger the cost of something then the more commission you get. But that doesn't mean you should neglect cheaper items which can easily sell.

You can look up any product that Amazon sells. Then all you have to do is get the link, just hit that. Boom, copy and paste this into your YouTube description or your website and from there, that's when you can start earning commission with Amazon Associates. When somebody clicks the link what happens is they get a cookie attached to their IP that lasts twenty four hours. Now here's the cool part, with Amazon if they buy anything within that twenty four hour period you actually get commission on every single thing that's in their cart. So it doesn't even have to be the product in your link.

So how do we take things a step further? This requires doing a little more work by creating an actual brand. Brands are important, and the best kind of brand is a personal brand. You can create a personal brand using YouTube which is a free platform. It doesn't cost you anything to make videos and upload them, it's all free. In addition create a website with blog posts and articles. What you can do is create a video on YouTube and also do an article on your website. It really isn't that hard to create a website blog. You can use WordPress, which is actually a free platform with some great themes. Then all you need is a domain and some web-hosting. Alternatively you can have someone build all that for you for a very reasonable price.

When you build that personal brand you can create something very powerful. We all have a story and a personality that we can share with the world. The plus side of this is that you get to build trust and a personal connection with your customers. If you were to just do the first method and you just review these things. You may get lucky and your video gets tens of thousands of views which can very well happen if you're reviewing something very popular. But where the real money starts to come in is when you become an authority figure. When people trust you, you have influence and people listen to what you have to say. So if you were to become an authority and you said that these are the best headphones of 2018 that I have tested then you guys are more likely to buy this, right?

Create consumer focused content. So what does this mean? I wouldn't be like, oh here's a link to my headphones. I would actually be like, hey guys, check it out. So I've owned twelve pairs of headphones within the last two years and these are by far my favorite Bluetooth headphones. They have perfect usability, the sound quality is amazing. Really tight sub bass and the Bluetooth and the battery life are excellent. You know what I mean? I would actually create a review, because a review gets people when they're in that phase of okay, I'm gonna go purchase a pair of headphones rather than if you're just watching a vlog of mine and I'm just like oh yeah, those are my headphones. You're not really likely to buy a $350 pair of headphones, right? So you want to create consumer focused content that really dials in when consumers are at that purchase decision when they're researching different products, they're comparing them, they're looking at reviews, that's where you want to capture your customer for the best chance of a sale.

Now the thing is, building a personal brand is not as hard as it seems. You can get started today, you don't have to be an expert. You just have to be passionate. You just have to be a person who's willing to give some valuable information to the next guy. You don't really have to do some crazy cinematics or anything like that. Once you get to a certain point of authority you can start to implement affiliate marketing by including affiliate links from Amazon Associates. Implement affiliate marketing into your personal brand and become an authority in your niche market.You should be aiming to become an authority figure in a market or niche. If you do that then you can create a very profitable website from something that you're passionate about. Now again, you don't have to really be an expert you just have to know enough to provide value to people. So for example, Beats, you don't have to be an audio expert to be able to recommend them to people who love hip hop. People who love bass, and who like that in your face sound quality, you know what I mean?

Share your hobbies and passions with the world. Once you got to a certain level, companies will started to send you their products for free in order to test out, So that's the other plus side of affiliate marketing and creating a brand is that when you build an asset like this companies come to you and they start giving you free stuff. So it's honestly a win-win, you start to earn passive income and you get freebies, I mean what's not to love? honestly creating that niche authority website, that brand really takes things to the next level. Really, if you want to succeed in this business you have to be thinking about the future.

Online courses are also a really good niche to become an affiliate for because the commissions are so high. Most of the commissions for online courses range from $100, $150, up to literally thousands of dollars for some of the really high end courses that cost $4000 and up. The good news is you don't have to be the expert because if you're someone who is a student then you can give just as much of a valid opinion as the next person. You bought the course, and you can give your actual valid opinion on it. Based on how you come across and what you say in that video you can sell a $1000 course and make a $400 commission. Basically, that's an easy way to make hundreds of dollars. If you're part of any courses right now. Honestly, just do a review on it. It doesn't even have to be all rainbows and butterflies. You can just be completely honest, throw it out there, who knows you might get a sale or two or three and boom, before you know it that's like $1000 right there.

You can also check out Clickbank Affiliate. This is similar to Amazon Affiliate, however they offer higher commissions of up to seventy five percent. In addition to focusing on physical products they also feature digital ones such as courses and tutorials. The profit per sale is very rewarding and you can earn significantly just through a few sales that click your affiliate link.

How To Make a Living On Fiverr

Fiverr is a market place where people sell their services or products from $5 upwards. There are strategies to increase the value and the amount that you can earn per sale by providing different upsells and additional add-ons as well.

To make money on Fiverr you can sell your own service or products. You might be good at something such as video editing, photo editing, graphic design, writing or any skill or service that is in demand. To give you more ideas, take a look through the categories on Fiverr.

There are a few factors that are crucial if you want to start making money on Fiverr. The first is the thumbnail of your gig. When you search for anything the thumbnail is the thing that stands out in the results. The more eye-catching and attractive the thumbnail is the more chances that someone is going to click on it and buy your gig. Test different thumbnails and see which one works best. Search in your category and look on the best-selling gigs and try to do something similar yet different.

The second most important factor is the description. You can go through your competition and have a look what kind of description they have. Analyze what works for them and do it in a similar way. Try to make it a little bit more personal, throw in a couple of jokes or something to stand out and not be as dry as your competitors. Videos can also really help convert your audience. Just explain what you do in the gig and make it more personable. You can make multiple gigs and try different descriptions and thumbnails for each to find the one that works the best.

Getting reviews is another the important factor that will define your success. Reputation on Fiverr is everything so if you see that the client is for example about to give you a bad review I recommend you to cancel the gig and this way you will save your reputation. You want to be aiming for five stars, one hundred percent, top reputation on Fiverr. This way people will have more trust in you and your gig will convert even better. Once you start getting the reviews and feedback, that's really going to boost you on Fiverr and help have your gig as a really popular premium gig. Fiverr will help promote your gigs if you have a really good service.

When you are all set, you can automate the entire Fiverr process and have a virtual assistant basically operate everything. That's the best position to be in, because then you're earning passive income. You're not going after active income where it always requires trading your time for money. With any business you still have to keep your eyes on it. You still have to oversee things, you still have to make sure things are converting and optimized.

Now how do you automate this process? Because doing a lot of these things requires a lot of time you might be wondering, how are these people on Fiverr doing this stuff for only $5? How are they really making money? When somebody would order the gig, have your virtual assistant send them an automated message with instructions on how they could get what they paid for in the gig. You can have your virtual assistant do that for you for as low as $3 an hour.

That's one way that you can automate it, and again, be able to earn profit to build a list or generate leads from. This could be sending them to another website to download information or see a video, for example. You can also upsell them on more things here such as a full course if you are just selling excerpts from it.

The key thing to success on Fiverr is to always provide more value than what people pay for. When you provide way more value they're going to become a raving fan, they're going to buy your other gigs, they're going to buy more from you and follow you on Fiverr and buy some additional things that you have as well.

How are you enjoying this book?
If you like it please share your thoughts and give it a review, thank you and enjoy the rest of the information.

How To Sell On Amazon FBA

Fulfillment by Amazon (FBA) is completely dominating the e-commerce industry. They are expanding every single day into new countries and territories. They are the absolute leader when it comes to e-commerce, which is a ridiculously high-growth industry. With Amazon FBA, they handle all of the hard work for you. You don't have to ship anything, you don't have to package anything, you don't have to create your own website and you don't have to accept payments. All of this is done by Amazon for you. So if you sell one unit a day or if you sell a thousand units a day there's no additional work on your behalf. Amazon's massive fulfillment warehouses handle this all for you and of course they take a fee for doing that, but it is well worth it.

Amazon have millions of customers and what that means for you being an Amazon seller is that you get a lot of free traffic coming to you. As long as you optimize your listing correctly and if you launch your product correctly it will show high up in the search results completely for free. You don't have to pay for that traffic which is one of the major benefits when it comes to actually selling on Amazon versus other types of e-commerce. There are five steps to being successful with Amazon FDA

Step One

Product research is the first step to finding the perfect product that is going to make you money. This is the absolute most vital step of the entire process. You can do everything else in the entire process poorly and you can still make a bunch of money. That is how good of a business model Amazon FBA is. But if you choose the wrong product, it becomes incredibly difficult to be successful on Amazon, no matter how good you are at creating a listing and marketing.

Amazon used to be a complete nightmare, looking through millions of different products literally could have taken weeks or months to do but there has been software services that have been released that take out all of the difficulty for you. The Viral Launch Tool allows you with a simple click of a button to apply a few filters and see exactly the products that you want to see with the criteria that you want. They have two pieces of software that are absolutely necessary when it comes to actually finding profitable products to sell on Amazon. The first piece of software is their web app. This goes through millions and millions of products on Amazon and you can apply different filters to actually see a specific product. So for example if you only want to see products in the baby section that have less than fifty reviews and sell on average more than $7,000 in revenue a month. Then you can literally put that into the filters and it will show you results that match. It will also give you ideas because there's such unbelievably random things that people sell on Amazon that are making thousands of dollars per month.

Essentially what you're looking for when doing product research is for products that have extremely low competition with a high amount of interest. It's the same thing as basic economics, a low amount of supply with a high level of demand. The main thing that we're looking for is products that have low reviews. Look for all the products on the page to have an average of less than fifty to seventy five reviews.

Another thing to look for is to make sure that everyone on page one has consistent revenue. If only one seller on page one of the search results has you know ten thousand dollars in revenue per month and everyone else has zero. Then maybe there's just not enough people actually searching for this particular product. For it to make sense you want to see consistent revenue and you want to see consistently low reviews. I recommend people going for products that have a monthly revenue of between seven and fifteen thousand dollars. Profit is usually about fifty percent of that but it starts to add up very quickly when you add new and profitable products to your product portfolio.

Next when doing product research you want to make sure of, is that the products that your thinking about selling are priced higher than thirteen dollars. The reason for that is that Amazon has fees for handling all of the hard work for you. If a product costs less than thirteen dollars what I've found is that Amazon's fees become too expensive. It takes up too much of your margin and thirteen dollars is about the lowest price that you can sell at as a new seller to actually be profitable. The highest price that I like look for is generally about fifty dollars. The reasoning behind this price range of thirteen to fifty dollars is people that don't recognize a brand are much less likely to make an impulse purchase if the product itself cost more than fifty dollars. The thirteen to fifty dollar range is generally the sweet spot. Remember Amazon is incredibly good at making you purchase things you didn't know that you actually needed to purchase. The entire website is designed to make you buy more things than you originally came to purchase. Therefore having a product that people are willing to buy on impulse is going to give you sales.

Last but not least, make sure that a product is not seasonal. For example Christmas stockings. These would have zero sales for eleven months a year and then have a massive spike. Look for a product with consistent demand throughout the entire year. The best tool to actually be able to see that is called Google Trends. This tool is completely free and it will tell you the average search volume and kind of popularity of any product or search term in the world over the entire year.

In summary, look for products on average that have less than fifty reviews, are priced between thirteen and fifty dollars, and are between seven and fifteen thousand dollars monthly revenue with consistent demand throughout the year. Some other things to keep in mind. Choose products that are non-breakable, small and light. so that they're not breaking in transit and not particularly complex if you have complex items people are much more likely to return them because they're not figuring out how to actually use it.

Step Two

Is finding the best supplier and actually getting that supplier to ship your product over to the USA so you can start selling them on Amazon. We're going to use a website called www.alibaba.com. Alibaba is a massive directory of all the manufacturers in China. They can literally make anything you could possibly imagine. Most of the things in your house and that anyone's wearing pretty much in the USA comes from China. Alibaba makes finding the manufacturer that you are looking for very easy. I recommend you to search by supplier. This means that you're not going to see a bunch of the same exact listings because one supplier might have a hundred product listings for the same product and if you search by product you're going to be reaching out and sending a hundred different emails to the same exact supplier. Looking by supplier will save you a bunch of time and your actually reaching out to multiple different suppliers which is very advantageous because you want to get at least three independent quotes on the product pricing.

When looking for supplier make sure to check a few things put. That they've been in business for a number of years. That they have a transaction history. That they have an online presence, a normal looking website and a phone number. To be on the safe side you can call the phone number just to make sure that they're a legitimate business. Some other things that you want to evaluate when you're talking to your supplier is how is their English, how fast are they responding and how good are they being with negotiation? You want to judge these things from the start because no two manufacturers are made equal and you want to choose the manufacturer that in the end is going to be the best long-term relationship for you both.

Once you've done some background research on your suppliers what you're going to do next is find the best three looking suppliers and you are going to ask them for a quote. One of them might give you a high price and the other a lower price. What you can then do is send the lowest quote to the others and say, hey I got this quote could you guys beat it? Oftentimes they'll come back with a better offer. Always try to negotiate the price down, which means directly more profit to your business.

Generally it takes between two and six weeks to actually get your product manufactured. So you want to factor that in when it comes to planning out when your products are actually going to arrive at Amazon. The first time you get your products manufactured generally takes a bit longer because you have to give them your logo, get your packaging design right and get the product up to spec. In addition you will get a sample sent to you which can take time as well.

The standard way that you pay a supplier is you deposit thirty percent for the entire order. Then only after they're finished and after your products have been inspected you send the last seventy percent. Inspections involve a third party or an independent party coming to the manufacturer who's making all of your products in China and say okay the products look good, the quality is there. They'll take samples and make sure everything looks completely one hundred percent ready to be shipped. Only after you actually have your product inspected do you pay that final seventy percent.

Always process payments through PayPal goods and services because you can get that money back if something goes wrong. If your supplier says they don't accept PayPal because it's more fees say okay we'll split the paypal fees 50/50. It's always worth it to do that if something goes wrong you're basically as protected as you can possibly be.

Step Three

Making a world-class, fully optimized Amazon listing. So before you can actually make a listing on Amazon you're going to have to set up your Amazon seller central account which is the platform that all sellers use to manage their inventory, to do their PPC and to create all of their listings. When you're setting up your Amazon seller central account what I recommend you do is actually choose the professional seller option. This is $39.99 per month but it allows you to sell as many units as you want every single month for no additional charge. If you choose the individual seller option you pay a one dollar fee every single time that you sell a product. So if you sell forty or less per month the individual plan probably makes sense for you. But you professional Amazon sellers people that intend to do this as a source of income are going to sell more than forty units a month.

To go about creating your product listing what you're going to do is, go to the create a new product listing section and then choose the relevant product category for your products. First of all is your product name which you need to fully optimize because it's very important from a search engine optimization perspective to have a lot of the keywords that your customers are going to eventually type into Amazon. Your title is paramount when it comes to actually ranking organically for all the search terms that your customers are going to potentially search. Next you put in your manufacturing name. This is the name that's going to actually show up as your seller store name on Amazon. Anytime you look for a product and click on a product listing in Amazon you can see the name of the sellers store right in blue over off to the right your brand name. You want to keep it fairly universal because later on you might want to expand into other things. Therefore naming your company something very specific is not a good thing in the long run. Name it something more general so you can have more products under your actual umbrella.

Next up your going to put in the product ID which is a universal product code (UPC). This is the actual numerical code that actually creates the barcode that's unique to every single product in the world. To be on the safe side I do recommend purchasing your barcodes as Amazon tends to prefer this. You need to then give your manufacturer the actual bar code that they are going to print on every single one of your products. How that generally works is you send them a PDF that has the barcode. They print off that PDF and put stickers on the outside of the box of each one of your units. What I recommend is having them actually apply it as a sticker to your product packaging. The reason for them actually printing it on the product packaging is because sometimes those printers aren't high enough quality and then later on down the line Amazon might not be able to actually scan it. Make sure that all of your boxes have made in China printed on them along with your logo and brand name, product barcode printed on a sticker and attached to each box as well product photography. If you want to be successful selling on Amazon don't be cheap when it comes to product photos

The next part is where you set your price. A lot of people make a mistake here and they'll set their price too low. Initially set your price at the highest possible amount you could ever see yourself selling your product. The reason for that is something called a price band restriction. So if you say for example you set your product price to $20, Amazon will not let you go higher but they will let you go down. So set your price at the highest you could ever realistically imagine yourself selling it and you can always lower it at any time. This will allow you to do special discounts and so on.

The last part of creating a fully optimized listing is making sure that your keywords are on point. How to research keywords? As an example let's say that your selling a garlic press. You would type in garlic into the Amazon search bar. Then you would see all of the related words to it because not everyone calls a garlic press a garlic press. Some people call it a garlic mincer some people call it you know a stainless steel garlic press or a jumbo garlic press. Overall what you're looking for here is all of the other highest volume search terms that somebody could type in wanting a garlic press. Add as many of those search terms to your bullet points, product description, title and of course to your back end keywords

Step Four

Is getting those first initial reviews and how to actually launch your product to page one. The only legitimate option when it comes to getting those first vital reviews is what is called, Amazon early reviewer program. It costs sixty US dollars and for that price Amazon incentivizes people to leave you a review. I recommend everyone to always participate in this program. For sixty dollars you get five reviews which equals about twelve dollars per review. That is a very good price to get reviews especially because it's so difficult now to actually get reviews any other way. The service is available in the advertising menu under Amazon early reviewer program. Always make sure that you have some reviews before you start your launch because think about it again logically. If you see a product on Amazon that has zero reviews are you going to buy it?

The next step is what's called the launch phase during which you have a promotion or a giveaway. First off you should generate coupon codes inside Amazon seller central. With these you would giveaway units of your product at a percentage off to people out there in the world who are couponers that want a good deal. If you sell more units per day Amazon's algorithm is going to say okay this product must be better, it's selling more let's rank it organically number one. Then more people will see it. The more units that sell, the more money Amazon makes and they want to obviously reward the people who are selling the most.

Step Five

Amazon Pay Per Click (PPC) is another powerful way to actually get additional sales and increase in your organic ranking for different keywords. There are two main options that you have available at your disposal for Amazon PPC. These are, automatic campaigns and manual campaigns. Automatic campaigns basically pull keywords from your listing and it takes all of those keywords and it automatically creates permutations of applicable keywords that it thinks people might be typing related to your listing. Automatic campaigns are extremely easy to create literally with a click of a button and Amazon does all of the hard work for you. The problem with automatic campaigns is generally they aren't as profitable because Amazon's testing a lot of things that aren't likely to work. To counter this, the strategy you can use with automatic campaigns is instead of creating one automatic campaign with fifty dollars per day, create ten automatic campaigns with five dollars per day. Then what you do is you pause all the ones that aren't performing and you scale up the daily spend of the ones that are performing.

For manual campaigns what you to do is you can look at the top performing sellers in any niche and you can find the exact words that they're ranking for and that they're using in their PPC campaigns. Then you can take those words and apply them to your own manual PPC campaigns.

Blog for a Living

What is a blog? Essentially a blog is a regularly updated page website. It is created and centered around regularly updated content and blog posts. The Huffington Post our BuzzFeed are both examples of websites that would mainly be considered a blog. Nowadays you can make a full-time income from blogging. However it's not easy and it's not an overnight success unless you're extremely lucky or you've got some really impressive connections.

Contrary to popular belief, blogs are not just an online diary about your thoughts. You can blog about whatever your heart desires, it can be company updates, a product you like, a workout you recommend to your friend or as a creative outlet to practice your writing a way to meet others and connect. There are infinite ways and infinite things that you can blog about it's really all up to you basically anything you can think.

When comes to getting traffic to your blog, the first thing to learn search engine optimization matters (SEO). SEO determines what shows up in the top of the rankings when you type in some phrase. You can pay to be in that top by using Google AdWords. Also showing to Google that you have a quality website through optimization and quality content will help you reach the top of the rankings.

To monetize your blog you can use Google AdSense. How this works is that you sign up for a free Google AdSense account, and then you get Google's code, you copy that, paste that into your website. Google will match which companies are willing to advertise for different search terms that are found on your site.

It's by far one of the easiest ways that you can monetize your site. All you have to do is write the content, copy and paste the code from Google AdSense, onto your site and then your done. To become more successful you need to have a high rank for these relevant search terms.

As you write more high quality content your traffic will increase. You want to be the first person to write about new things in your niche. Networking with other bloggers will give you a clear view of what's going to happen in the future. Ask yourself what is potentially going to change in my category that no one else has wrote about yet? You can be the second or third person but if you publish a good piece of content that's better than anything else out there, then you can potentially outrank them, and also get more social shares out of it.

Another income stream you can add to your blogging is to incorporate affiliates. With affiliate marketing you're representing a company that offers a product or service that you believe in, preferably one that you've tried out yourself. If you write about them and mention them on your blog and if one of your readers clicks that link, and then opens an account with that affiliate or buys a product through that link from that affiliate then you get paid a small commission. Make sure you're representing affiliates that you believe in, that you trust. If you're just signing up to be an affiliate for some company just to earn a quick buck, your readers are going to know.

How are you enjoying this book?
If you like it please share your thoughts and give it a review, thank you and enjoy the rest of the information.

Udemy Course Creation

If you're somebody who is thinking about teaching online or wants to get involved with it then creating your own online courses with Udemy is a great way to start. If you put in enough time, energy and effort you can definitely gain great financial results. It can eventually become a passive income stream where you can probably spend less than fifteen minutes a week on it. Udemy does a lot to promote your courses and they currently have over twelve million students on their platform so it's kind of a built-in audience.

When starting out the first step is the production of the course. For beginners you can use some basic video and microphone equipment. Smartphones are pretty good for video these days, but make sure you get a decent microphone for the audio. You can tape up a piece of paper as a makeshift teleprompter underneath the camera. Plan out your course with some slides or live footage, depending on your subject. Try to mix it up with screen sharing segments or PowerPoint segments where you are walking through an actual process. Add in screen share shots like talking head stuff and even written parts, quizzes and so on. Mix up the content so that its not just you lecturing in from the camera for five hours because that would probably generate some negative feedback. Try to make your segments around two to ten minutes long. Keeping lectures short makes it feel like it's building momentum for the students going through your course.

With marketing it's really similar to Amazon in that you know when you're launching a book you have to give it that initial marketing push and then let the algorithm try and take notice.

Try to generate a critical mass of enrollments of students and reviews because both of those metrics are pretty prominent on the sales page. You can create free coupons to send out to your peers, colleagues and other authors. Say, hey check this out here's a free coupon and if you like it, drop in a review. Also share the coupons in Facebook coupon groups and on coupon sites. At the start you can also set the course price for free. Aim for about one thousand enrollments and then set your price. Interact with your students, send them welcome notices and keep them engaged with course updates. If your content it good then they are more likely to buy your other courses. You should always be creating more courses and improving along the way.

Finally, if you have a podcast, YouTube channel or online presence you can share your course there.

Build & Optimize A Professional Shopify

Creating a drop shipping company is one of the best business models for beginners using Shopify. If you've ever bought something from Ebay there's a chance that you bought it from someone drop shipping. You don't have to invest money up front and Shopify does all the hard design work for you.

First off sign up with Shopify and choose a store name. The store name will appear in the free domain that Shopify is going to give you. Next you are going to choose a product on a website called Aliexpress. This is a Chinese website where suppliers sell directly. You can find many cheap products that are still good quality. You are going to list the same product with the same images and description on your ecommerce store that you are going to create with Shopify. Obviously you will list it on your store for a higher price. Whenever you receive an order you confirm the payment and the customers address. Then you go to Aliexpress, order the product and ship it directly to the customer and you keep the difference.

You can do it wherever you are in the world as long as you have an internet connection and a computer. Aliexpress ships to the United States without you having to touch any of the items. You don't have to do anything, just press a button. You might be thinking, can the customer go directly on Aliexpress and order that product by themselves? Yes they can but in ninety nine percent of the cases people want simplicity because most people don't even know Aliexpress exists and also people buy from where it's most familiar and convenient.

When it comes to selecting a product there are some fundamental things you need to be aware of. If you get this right then you are going to be successful with Shopify. Whatever niche you choose, make sure it is a passionate niche. In fact there's a big difference between what people need and what people are passionate about. When people need something they go on Amazon and buy from there. They don't even think about your Shopify store. However if you sell something unique and interesting that people are passionate about then you are going to have success. Here are some examples of niches that people have passion for. People really love their pets, obviously there is a dog niche divided into many different sub niches. People that own a Labrador, a golden retriever or whatever dog breed. You can find t-shirts and accessories for those specific people. The golf niche is very passionate and people usually have plenty of money. Camping and survival people really love these activities and buy these gear and accessories. Gardening, cycling, hiking, fishing, all these activities and sports people, they love doing them. Be a little bit creative and find products that these people might enjoy and want to buy. The best way to do this is to actually combine these niches. For example if you want to get into the cat niche then you want to find accessories and jewelry related to cats. In this way you're targeting a specific audience who loves cats but they also love jewelry, bracelets, necklaces or whatever.

For more ideas use Aliexpress and check the categories section. You will find that there are many categories and many, many subcategories. For example, jewelry, necklaces and pendants, rings, trendy earrings, bracelets, bangles etc. Once you find a product you can import all the details to your Shopify store.

There are two things that you have to check for when choosing a product on Aliexpress. The first one is the shipping, look for quick and cheap. Most suppliers offer free shipping, but one to two dollars is fine. When shipping to The United States it's usually quite fast, between twelve to twenty days. For The United Kingdom you'll see that it's usually at least twenty to forty days. Avoid all the shippings that are over twenty days. The customers will be upset, therefore sending to The United States is always the easiest and cheapest option.

The second thing you have check is the seller rating. To do this in the search page, move your mouse over a product and see the icons that appear. We always want to find products that have at least three diamonds and less than four crowns. In this range sellers are established and reliable but still not too premium and so the prices are still reasonable. Products with five crowns are a little bit more expensive. Always avoid the medals because these are new sellers or maybe they have bad reviews so stay away from them. Price wise I recommend products from zero to ten dollars on Aliexpress so that you can resell them from five to thirty dollars on your Shopify store.

When you have chosen a product you will need to then design and customise your Shopify store. First of all install a theme. The theme is basically controlling how your website looks. You can then customize this to display your products, text and images as you prefer. Add a countdown timer because scarcity is a very powerful sales method. When a product is available for a limited time customers are more likely to buy immediately. You can explore the app store and find hundreds of apps for your Shopify store. In the beginning you want to keep it simple and start with a few apps and then when you are making money there is no problem in buying more apps.

Traffic is the lifeblood of your business. You can have the most beautiful store in the world but if you don't send traffic to it, then you won't make any money. There are two ways to send traffic to your website. The first one is to pay for the traffic and the second one is to use free traffic methods. When you use paid traffic you have complete control over it and also it's reliable and predictable. While if you don't have any money there are free traffic methods but you have less control over them. Most people get scared of using paid traffic because they think they have to invest thousands of dollars. It's crazy how people are not willing to invest a few bucks in something that could potentially make them thousands of dollars. There are so many traffic sources where you can buy traffic. The most popular is Facebook and with over two billion users the potential is huge. You don't need a huge budget, you can start with three or more dollars a day. Create and install the Facebook pixel in your Shopify store to enable this.

Instagram influencers can also help promote your store. Try to find people with a big following in your niche. Instead of paying them up front you can offer to share revenue so that you don't have to invest anything. You can also use paid Google adverts to rank for keywords relevant to your niche. When someone searches for your products your store should be near the top of the first page of results.

Ghost Production: Make Money from Your Music

If your a music producer with some hot beats you can easily make money online with ghost producing. Ghost producing essentially is making songs and then selling them to other people. There are different levels, at one extreme you're making songs for people and just selling the songs to them that they can then repackage up and market as their own. Then at the other extreme you're basically helping someone on a track without getting explicit credit in the track title. You may even get credit in the official release notes or as a featured artist on the actual track.

To get started make lots and lots of commercially viable songs. If you're working in an obscure genre that doesn't have a lot of money flowing into it then there will be less successful and rich people who would be interested to buy your music. If you want to make decent money then you need to follow the money.

You can sell your music at sites such as the following:

https://www.edmghostproducer.com
Connecting up and coming DJs with Ghost Producers, EDM Ghost Producer is the perfect intermediate for both buying and selling custom made tracks online.

https://www.ghostproducing.com
Produce original or remix according to your ideas. Do you need help about finishing your music? We can finish it for you and turn it to a quality class music!

https://houseoftracks.com/
Build a career from music production. Sell your tracks to a huge customer base.

Upwork and Fiverr are also great websites where you can offer your music and music production services.

A further step you can take is to proactively reach out to people who might be in the position to purchase a song. At the one extreme you might have a sort of popular DJ and at the other extreme you have something more interesting a celebrity. Have you seen how many sort of TV actors and sort of personalities in the world also do DJing? Now most of these celebrity DJ's don't actually release music currently but they should do and that's where you come in as the ghost producer. What you can do is approach the manager of this celebrity. This is where you need a lots of tracks because if you just come to them with one track and you say this is my track, do you want to buy it? Then they're going to say no probably because music is subjective.

So what you need to do is approach them with at least five different tracks and then hopefully they'd like a few or just even one of your tracks. Then ideally what will happen are a few things. One option is they just like it as it is and they will just buy it or offer you some sort of like royalty for work. If they offer you royalties then that's great because you will get a consistent revenue from any sales. Another option is maybe they like most of it but wants a little bit of a tweak and that's absolutely cool.

The potential money that can be earned from ghost producing is huge. Some hip hop ghost producers are known for charging fees of fifteen thousand dollars and up for a song. For beginners five hundred dollars is a good start.

YouTube: Monetize & Attract More Viewers

Youtube is a great way to earn money online. If your someone who has a lot of followers online then there's a few different ways to bring in revenue. One is through monetizing your videos and getting paid through Advertising with Google Adsense. Recently YouTube has changed the rules to join the program. In the past adverts were showing up on videos that weren't really advertiser friendly. Nowadays you need a minimum of four thousand hours of watch time and a minimum of one thousand subscribers.

To be successful with Adsense on YouTube the key strategy would be to get a lot of views. The advertising revenue is basically going off that the more views you get the more money you make. Therefore if you want to earn a decent income then you must make content that will bring in lots of views. Every time someone watches one of your videos, adverts will appear either on the sides of the videos, before it starts or sometimes in the middle of a video. These adverts are what will earn you money, and sometimes people don't even need to click on them for you to still make a profit from them.The typical pay rate is two dollars for every thousand views. So if your goal is to earn a thousand dollars extra, you would need a half a million views to get a thousand dollars. But don't worry, the good news is there's tons of people crushing it that have small views but they're monetizing in other ways. One thing you can do with YouTube adverts is if you really niche your channel down and go into certain niches that have higher click through, you can start earning some decent money.

The second way to earn money with YouTube is affiliate marketing. You can start getting custom links from Amazon Associates or other affiliate programs and paste them into your YouTube video description and then you can make money when someone clicks the link (see Affiliate Marketing chapter for more information). The next way to monetize your YouTube Channel is through brand deals, whether that means a sponsored video or a shout-out in a video. When working with a brand, never work with a product you do not believe in or message you don't agree with. Once you start trying to sell you it can sometimes end up devaluing your content and in turn devaluing that brand.

Remember, YouTube will often go through multiple phases and algorithm changes that affects a lot of smaller creators revenue. Keep up to date with the changes and adapt as required.

Make Money With Envato

Envato is the world's largest digital assets provider. Everything is available here including, web templates, code, photos, videos, music, presets and much more. You could for example sell your codes for some apps or some software anything or maybe some video graphics or Photoshop templates. There are so many options, for ideas head over to Envato and see what is selling now.

As a case study, you might design a website template and sell it on Envato for fifty dollars, a thousand times in a year and make some real money. The reality is this you have the ability to sell it as many times as possible throughout the entire lifetime of that piece of intellectual property. It's a practical time investment to make a product or something that can be resold multiple times. Therefore make the extra effort to make products that you can resell. You can even buy intellectual rights for some products and sell them. It could also maybe a variation of that. Essentially your selling that and making some great passive income.

You might want to check out Envato if you're a creative person and skilled with different softwares, making music, or videos. For example, you can create templates for wordpress sites through Envato's themeforest, and every time someone decides to go with your creations you will get paid. If you're skilled with creating music, upload some sick tunes and you will create a passive income stream if people buy your tunes. If you have great photography skills or design skills, share them there.

Envato also offer an affiliate program. You can sign up for this and when your done find any Envato products, then just paste your link and share where you want to promote.

How are you enjoying this book?
If you like it please share your thoughts and give it a review, thank you and enjoy the rest of the information.

Setup A Successful Patreon

Patreon is a membership platform that makes it really easy for creators to get paid. It is a crowdsourcing type of income model that's based entirely around rewards and incentives that you the content creator get to design for your own audience. The concept comes from the idea of patronage which is actually a really old idea. Mozart, Shakespeare and Da Vinci they all had patrons, mostly aristocrats who paid them to create so they could enjoy their works and brag to their friends about how cool they are for supporting creators. In essence it's kind of like that but better because this provides creators with a sustainable income while retaining creative control and it allows fans to connect with them on a whole new level. So if you're a professional creator start a page and give your fans the opportunity to become patrons. Different people are trying to find a way to monetize their creative content and keep pursuing the things that they're passionate about. Patreon offers a great to do that and it could help you create the best work of your life.

Assuming you have a following and people are fans of what you do, you can set up a Patreon account and let your fans subscribe to you. They can then decide on how much they want to donate to you. When you sign up you'll be greeted by a display name. I highly recommend using something that you use on your page, or your book, or your album or wherever you're producing content. Whatever name you go by there have it be the same name here on Patreon. It's just going to make it much easier to find you. You're also going to have a profile picture. This is the same type of profile picture that you have on your YouTube channel or wherever else you are. You really want your cover image to reflect your personality and what you do in the best possible way. Maybe that's just having a thing that says your brand with the times you stream or the times you release videos, or something else entirely. Be creative.

Next you're going to have some social media links. Include all of the social media, the more the better. Facebook, YouTube, Instagram, Twitter all that stuff, include it. Next, move to your About section. This is huge, think of this as your sales pitch. It is the only opportunity you have to convince someone to invest their hard-earned money in you and your creative products. This should be a short little paragraph about what people can expect from you but way more important than just this text part is your intro video. This is not an introduction of your YouTube channel or book or twitch or short stories. This is an introduction of Patreon to your existing audience on whatever platform they are on. While Patreon does have a really great search function, the majority of your new Patrons are not going to come from the website itself. Instead they'll come from the traffic that you kick up on your platform where they already know you.

Just as important as the About section is your reward tiers. This is what sets Patreon apart from YouTube or Twitch or other crowdsourcing sites. You can create as many or as few tiers as you choose and you get to create them specifically for your own audience which is different than any other audience on earth. You should use that to your advantage when creating these reward tiers. The most important thing is not to create more work for yourself. Writing a personalized thank you message for every patron might sound like a great idea but when your Patreon starts booming and you have to create a hundred individual thank you messages you aren't spending time doing the thing people are paying you to begin with.

The best reward tiers you can design are ones that happen alongside the work you are already doing. Such as creating credits at the end of a video or using people's names and short stories. Think about what you want from your favorite creator or what you would want from your favorite creator because believe it or not you are somebody's favorite. It's very important to put yourself in others shoes while designing these reward tiers. Finally don't make too many reward tiers, too many choices and people will tend to get overwhelmed. It's more important that you feel like people are getting an adequate reward then for you to have a ton of reward tiers. If you have the perfect hundred dollar tier don't be afraid to use it, honestly the reward far outweighs the amount.

Finally after setting up everything you have one last thing to do and that is to set up your goals. Start small and attainable, people will want to help you reach those goals. If you start with something crazy and unattainable or not entirely realistically, people might not want to waste their money and see you not reach that goal. People are more likely to spend the money if you are close to the goal or if they can have a significant contribution to the goal. Update these goals often and be sure to include rewards in these goals for all the patrons who helped you reach it.

Take your time before the launch of your Patreon. Make sure everything is exactly how you want it and remember never give up.

Bonus: Why People Fail Online

There are three main reasons why people fail to make money online. This all revolves around one similar theme and that is a lack of focus. You can be as lazy as you want but if you're unfocused you're not going to be successful with making money online.

Reason One

What often will happen as a beginner is you will have a tendency to jump from one method to another. So if you're here right now because you want to learn affiliate marketing, at some point you're going to get distracted and you're going to go after mobile marketing or you might consider creating a YouTube channel. There are literally hundreds of different ways to make money online, way more than in this book. Now as a beginner you have to figure out what's best for you. So during your beginning phase it's all about figuring out which of the ways to make money online is best for you. Maybe you work full time and have a few hours spare or you recently quit your job. Figure out what works best for you. You should try a few ideas but eventually you need to cut that out and stick with one thing that you like, that works for you. When you stick with one it is your job is to master that one.

Reason Two

People tend to give up right before they find the diamond. There is a famous story about a guy who started a mining company. He bought all this equipment, got loans from friends and family and then he started digging a hole in this spot that he thought had gold in it. About ten feet down he found some gold so he started pressing on farther and farther. He went down to almost three hundred feet, without finding any more gold so he gave up and he folded the company. Three years later someone else went back to that exact same hole and dug three feet down farther than the guy did before and that's when they found one of the biggest gold mines in the history of that particular state. On the internet this story is very common, people get so far and reach that breaking point. Then because of emotions and lack of faith in their method they give up right before they start making a lot of money. This happens all the time, so if that's you, make sure you continue to push through. Check out other stories of people working in the same field for inspiration. You will be surprised and you can relate with their struggles.

Reason Three

You find a winning income stream and for whatever reason decide it will be best to let that go and keep it earning steady while you try and find something else. Maybe it's another niche, or another method. So what will happen is this first thing keeps making money but eventually because your focus is now elsewhere the income starts to drop and eventually goes away. What you should do is, once you find that one winning thing it doesn't matter if it's a one affiliate site or a YouTube channel. Once you find that one winner you have to hammer away at that winner until there's nothing left for you to gain anymore. Alright, so that means you keep creating content, you keep creating videos, try to get some paid at traffic in there, try to create your own products. Once you get that winner hammer that thing out until there is nothing left for you to gain from it.

Ok, so keep that in mind those are the three main reasons people fail.

Stay focused, persistent and think positive about your future.

I wish you all the best.

Bonus: Inspirational Stories

Kelly, 26 Years Old. Former Truck Driver

I've had two main jobs and in my life which were pretty grueling. I didn't have a whole lot of hope for my future. I had dropped out of college a couple times because I'm one of those personality types. I have a hard time making myself do something that I really don't like. I didn't have a lot of interest in college so I just could not make myself go with it. Then I chained myself nine to five employment. My first job was a call center worker. If any of you that have a call center background of tech support or customer service support then you know that can be pretty grueling. After a couple years of that I became a truck driver. I was just really looking for things to get me out of the call center position. I saw the idea of becoming a team truck driver because I really needed a change in my life and you can actually make some good money as a truck driver. To briefly summarize the truck driving experience, let's just say a week or two on the road had me wanting to go back to the call center. You live in the truck, they don't really even want you to stop to stock up on food like at Walmart they want you to just stop eat at the truck stops and that's why you see so many unhealthy truckers. It's really a road to the bottom faster than you wouldn't believe.

I just couldn't take it so after four months I quit. I had a decent amount of money but was still pretty depressed feeling like my life wasn't really going anywhere. It felt like I will live in a cycle of poverty for the rest of my life if I did not make a change. So I tried to make money online. Actually I had tried that on and off since I was twenty years old but that time I was still lazy and not ready to devote myself. This time I was more serious. I got involved with some courses on how to make money online. I threw myself into the training and I followed everything that the training said to do. Everyday I took action and actually stuck with it, day in and day out. I remember making my first little bit and then being inspired and growing it.

During that time i had gone back to the call center job to make sure my income was stable. But after one year I actually quit my job when I started to make good money online. I haven't looked back, I mean basically I just kept doing what I was doing. I devoted myself to it and followed a routine.

If I didn't make that change and choose to learn how to make money online I was gonna go into my later years stuck in the cycle of poverty. I just made the decision no more no more. When you decide to turn that switch on it is what's going to completely transform your life

Steve, 34 Years Old. Former Fitness Instructor

A year and a half ago I worked at LA Fitness. I've always fought with this idea that I wanted to work for myself, be my own boss because I just hate being you know told to do stupid things by people that I don't really respect. I got really tired of that at my last job. I remember there was a time I had to work two weeks straight with no days off. I was miserable and I didn't like what I was doing. That really made me open my eyes to the reality that have to work smart because I saw guys there making $40,000 but they were putting in like a 9:00 in the morning to 10:00 at night sometimes just dealing with all sorts of crap. I got so tired of it and seeing them what I realized is I was looking at them and I was like these guys are working really hard but they're not really doing anything. The flurries of activity where you know you're doing a lot of stuff but it's not really getting you anywhere you're not being smart about what you're doing.

Moving forward on time I enrolled in a social media marketing agency program. What that is in short is you run social media for small businesses that are not very known on social media like a little restaurant or a little salon or whatever it is and you help them get traffic. They pay you per month to run that social media and I got into that. After some time I ran into this barrier where I didn't like social media marketing I was like maybe there's just something wrong with me like I'm being too whiny or I'm just I need to just get over it or whatever. I felt like this is still not right for me.

Later on I found out about selling on Amazon and I was so excited because you could make money online but you didn't have to sell you never even have to talk on the phone. I took courses to speed up my learning curve tremendously. My business grew fast as I gained more knowledge. I was inspired by the results and it just keeps growing.

Eventually I was able to quit my fitness job and now work for myself.

Thanks for Reading!

What did you think of, **Make Money Online: Twelve Proven Methods To Earn Passive Income And Work From Anywhere in the World**

I know you could have picked any number of books to read, but you picked this book and for that I am extremely grateful.

I hope that it added at value and quality to your everyday life. If so, it would be really nice if you could share this book with your friends and family by posting to Facebook and Twitter.

If you enjoyed this book and found some benefit in reading this, I'd like to hear from you and hope that you could take some time to post a review. Your feedback and support will help this author to greatly improve his writing craft for future projects and make this book even better.

I want you, the reader, to know that your review is very important and so, if you'd like to leave a review, all you have to do is click here and away you go. I wish you all the best in your future success!

Also check out my other book:

Evernote: Master the Powerful New Way to Organize Projects and Optimize Productivity - Collect, Share, and Grow Ideas

Thank you and good luck!

Max Lane 2018

www.ingramcontent.com/pod-product-compliance
Lightning Source LLC
Chambersburg PA
CBHW031910200326
41597CB00012B/571